American★Girl Library®

Great Girl Food

Easy Eats & Tempting Treats
For Girls to Make

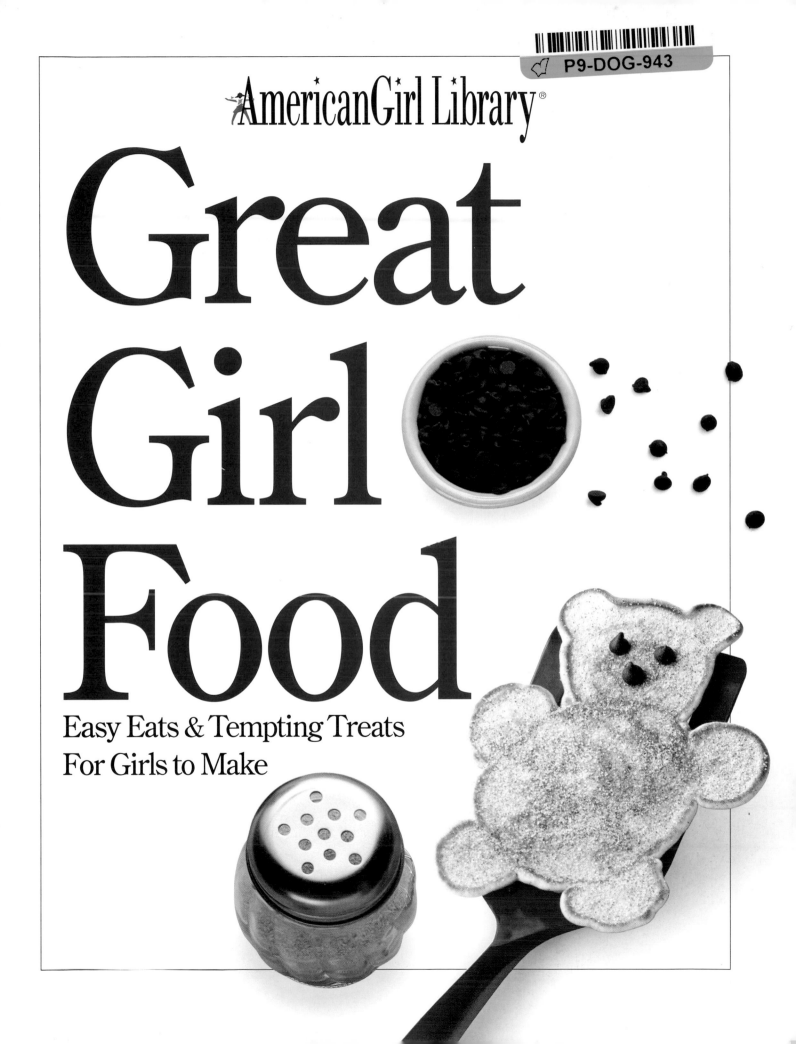

Published by Pleasant Company Publications
© Copyright 1996 by Pleasant Company

First Edition.
Printed in the United States of America.
96 97 98 99 WCR 10 9 8 7 6 5 4 3 2 1

American Girl Library® is a trademark of Pleasant Company.

Recipe Development and Food Styling: Bonnie Rabert
Editorial Development: Andrea Weiss
Art Direction: Kym Abrams
Design: Amy Hynous
Photography: Mike Walker, Paul Tryba, Alan Shortall
Illustration: Judy Pelikan

Portions of this book have previously been published in
American Girl® magazine.

Library of Congress Cataloging-in-Publication Data
Great girl food : easy eats & tempting treats for girls to make /
    illustrated by Judy Pelikan. — 1st ed.
        p. cm. — (American girl library)
Summary: Easy recipes for girls to make for daily meals and
    special occasions.
ISBN 1-56247-483-9
1. Cookery—Juvenile literature. [1. Cookery.] I. Pelikan, Judy,
ill. II. Series: American girl library (Middleton, Wis.)
TX652.5.G715 1996   641.5—dc20   96-13744 CIP AC

★American★Girl Library®

Great
Girl
Food

Easy Eats & Tempting Treats
For Girls to Make

PLEASANT
COMPANY
PUBLICATIONS™

Contents

Getting Started 6

Learning the Basics 8

Good Morning Meals

Breakfast Bowls 10

Cinnamon Bears 12

Egg-stra Special Eggs 14

Scrumptious Lunches

Cowgirl Lunch 16

Safari Lunch 18

Grab Bags to Go 20

Snack Attack!

Mix 'n' Match Handfuls 22

Warm Up, Cool Down! 24

Super Suppers

Spaghetti Pie 26

1 Potato, 2 Potato 28

Pizza Your Way 30

Sweet Treats

Potted Pudding 32

Less-Mess Cake 34

Flower Cookies 36

Celebrate!

Homemade Valentines 38

Tricky Treats 40

Sleepover Pleasers 42

Frosty Holiday Scene 45

Terms & Tools 48

Getting Started

The more prepared you are, the easier it is to make great food anytime.

Be a Smart Shopper

You have to start with good ingredients to get good results.

- Before shopping for ingredients, first check to see what you already have at home. Then write down exactly what you still need and how much. That way you won't waste food, and you won't have to make extra trips to the store for things you forgot.

- Know what's in what you eat. Read packages carefully, especially if you are looking for foods without too much fat or sugar. Sometimes pictures make the food look better or healthier than it really is, so check the list of ingredients to see what's really in it. And some brands taste better than others. You may have to try different brands to find the ones you like.

- Pick fresh foods carefully. Fruit should be soft but not mushy or bruised. You should be able to smell the flavor. Vegetables should look crisp, not spotted or wilted. Beef should look bright red, not gray or brown. Most fresh meat, milk, cheese, eggs, and other dairy products have an *expiration date* on them to tell you how long the food will keep before spoiling. Check this date so you don't buy something that will spoil before you can use it.

Be Safe!

This symbol means you'll need special help from an adult. Of course, always follow your family kitchen rules, and remember to:

- Work with sleeves rolled up, hair back, and apron strings tied.
- Wash hands, utensils, and work surfaces with hot, soapy water before and after handling food, especially raw meat.
- Carry knives point down. Don't leave them near the edges of counters or tables.
- Use thick, dry oven mitts for handling anything on the stove, in the oven, or out of the microwave.
- Remove pot lids carefully, tilted away from you so the steam doesn't scald.
- Turn pot handles toward the wall, not toward hot burners or over the edge of the stove where they can be bumped.
- Wipe up spills right away.
- When using an electric mixer, keep fingers out of the bowl and utensils away from the blades.
- Never plug in appliances with wet hands. Turn off appliances as soon as you're finished with them.

Plan Ahead

You'll thank yourself later.

- Before you start to make any recipe, carefully read the directions and the list of ingredients. Make sure you understand everything and have what you need.
- Figure out how much time you need, including cooling time, so you don't find out too late that you should have started sooner!
- Get out all of the tools and ingredients you'll be using. Make sure you have a dish towel or sponge nearby to wipe up spills quickly.
- Check to see if you need to preheat the oven.

7

Learning the Basics

Cutting Vegetables

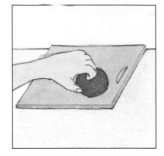

1 Place the vegetable on the cutting board. Hold the vegetable with the hand you don't write with, keeping your fingertips tucked under.

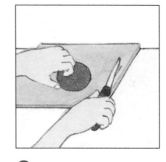

2 Hold the knife in your writing hand by "shaking hands" with the handle.

3 Place the blade of the knife across the top of the vegetable. Draw the knife down and back toward you to make a slice.

Cracking an Egg

1 Hold the egg in one hand. Tap the middle of it gently but firmly against the side of the bowl.

2 Hold the egg over the bowl, cracked side down, with your thumbs along each side of the crack. Carefully pull apart the shell and let all of the egg flow out.

3 Check for bits of eggshell in the bowl. Scoop them up with one of the eggshell halves. This works better than a spoon because the shell sticks to the tiny pieces instead of making them "squirt" away.

Be careful, follow the directions, and learn from your mistakes, and you'll be a kitchen pro in no time.

Measuring Liquid Ingredients

HELPFUL HINT

Use a glass or other clear measuring cup. For measuring less than ¼ of a cup, use measuring spoons.

1 Place the measuring cup on an even surface. Pour the liquid into the cup.

2 Bend down so your eye is exactly even with the measurement mark you are using. The liquid should be level with this mark. If it isn't, add or pour out liquid and check it again.

Amounts

a pinch =
less than ¼ teaspoon

a dash = a few drops

3 teaspoons = 1 tablespoon

2 tablespoons =
1 liquid ounce

4 tablespoons =
2 liquid ounces = ¼ cup

8 tablespoons =
4 liquid ounces = ½ cup

1 cup = ½ pint =
8 liquid ounces =
16 tablespoons

2 cups = 1 pint (liquid) or
1 pound (dry) = 16 ounces

4 cups = 2 pints = 1 quart =
32 liquid ounces

4 quarts = 1 gallon

Measuring Dry Ingredients

HELPFUL HINT

Use the scooping type of measuring cup for things like sugar and flour. For measuring less than ¼ of a cup, use measuring spoons.

1 Lightly scoop up the ingredient to fill the cup or spoon. Don't pack it in, unless you are measuring brown sugar. Then you should pack it tightly.

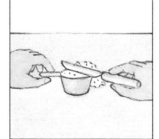

2 With the edge of a butter knife or metal spatula, scrape evenly across the top of the cup or spoon to remove the excess ingredient.

For measuring chopped nuts, vegetables, or other foods, you can use either kind of measuring cup.

Breakfast Bowls

Rainbow Banana Split

YOU WILL NEED

Ingredients

- 1 cantaloupe wedge
- 1 honeydew melon wedge
- 1 watermelon wedge
- 3 tablespoons of vanilla or fruit-flavored yogurt
- 1 banana
- 1 tablespoon of granola or fruit-flavored dry cereal
- 3 strawberries

Equipment

- Ice cream scoop
- Oval-shaped dish
- Spoon
- Table knife

Here's the Scoop

Use an ice cream scoop to scrape out long, thin strips of melon. The strips will curl into balls.

Creamy Combinations

Spoon on your favorite flavor of yogurt, or swirl different ones together—try strawberry and banana, or vanilla and blueberry.

Why settle for just plain flakes or fruit? Serve up spoonfuls of smiles instead!

Sidesplitting!

Peel a banana and cut it down the middle lengthwise. Place the banana halves along the sides of the dish.

Top It Off

Add some dry cereal for crunch, and crown your creation with 3 sweet strawberries.

Whirlygig

Warm up to a bowl of hot cereal with a sweet, swirly twist.

1 Stir 1 tablespoon of strawberry preserves in a bowl until it turns runny. (You may have to mush up or take out the big pieces of fruit.)

2 Make a bowl of your favorite hot cereal, following the directions on the package.

3 Drizzle the preserves onto the cereal in a spiral design. Add blueberries on top.

Another Twist: Trade the strawberry preserves for a swirl of maple syrup, applesauce, chocolate sauce, or your favorite flavor of jam.

Cinnamon Bears

Give someone you love a special wake-up call with these grizzly griddle cakes and a big bear hug.

YOU WILL NEED

♥ **An adult to help you**

Ingredients

- 6 tablespoons butter
- 3 tablespoons sugar
- ¼ teaspoon cinnamon
- 1 egg
- 1 cup flour
- ¼ cup "quick" oats
- 1 teaspoon baking powder
- 1 cup club soda
- Chocolate chips

Equipment

- Butter knife
- Microwavable dish
- Waxed paper
- Measuring spoons
- Measuring cups
- Mixing bowls
- Fork or wire whisk
- Electric griddle or heavy skillet
- Spatula
- Cooling rack
- Pastry brush

1 Cut up the butter and put it in the microwavable dish, covered with waxed paper. Microwave on HIGH for 45–60 seconds. In a small mixing bowl, mix the sugar and cinnamon.

2 Beat the egg. Combine it with the flour, oats, baking powder, 1 tablespoon of cinnamon-sugar mix, 2 tablespoons of melted butter, and club soda. Whisk until smooth.

3 ♥ Heat the griddle to MEDIUM HIGH or 375 degrees. If you drop water on the surface, it should "dance" and disappear. Drizzle some melted butter onto the griddle.

4 ♥ To make each bear, scoop some batter into a measuring cup. Slowly pour about 2 tablespoons onto the griddle to make the bear's body. Pour about 1 tablespoon for the head. Drip batter at the top and sides to form ears and paws.

5 ♥ When the edges look cooked and golden brown underneath, flip the bear shapes over and cook the other side. When done, remove the pancakes to the cooling rack.

6 Brush the pancakes with melted butter, and sprinkle some cinnamon-sugar mix on top. Then add chocolate chips to make the eyes and noses. Serve while still warm and cuddly!

Batter up!

For a faster way to make the batter, combine 1 cup of prepared pancake mix with ¼ cup quick (not instant or old-fashioned) oats and 1 cup club soda.

Egg-stra Special Eggs

Give a toast to these unbeatable eggs—served up just the way you like 'em!

YOU WILL NEED

🖐️ **An adult to help you**

Ingredients
- 1 teaspoon of soft margarine
- 1 slice of white or whole wheat bread
- 1 egg

Equipment
- Butter knife
- 3-inch cookie cutter or drinking glass
- Frying pan with lid
- Small bowl
- Spatula

1 Spread margarine on each side of the slice of bread.

2 With the cookie cutter or drinking glass, cut a hole out of the middle of the slice.

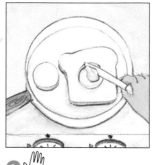

3 🖐️ Heat the frying pan on MEDIUM. Place the slice and the cutout piece in the pan. Put a little margarine inside the hole.

4 🖐️ Break the egg into the small bowl. Gently pour it into the hole in the slice. Cover the pan and cook 2 minutes.

5 🖐️ With the spatula, flip the slice and the cutout piece. Put the cover on and cook until the bottom is browned and the egg is almost set (not runny anymore).

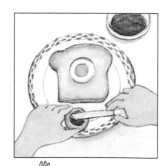

6 🖐️ Remove the slice and cutout piece from the pan. For a touch of sweetness, spread the cutout piece with your favorite jelly or preserves.

Omelette in the Middle

Beat the egg. Add salt and pepper, 1 tablespoon of chopped ham or bacon, and 1 teaspoon of chopped green onion. Place the buttered bread in the pan. Pour in about half the egg mixture. Save the rest for another serving. Cook, covered, for 2 minutes. Flip and cook, covered, until the egg is almost set.

Scrambled Around

Fry the bread on 1 side and turn over. Beat the egg and pour half of it in the hole. Use the rest for another serving. As the egg cooks, stir with the corner of a rubber spatula.

Over Easy

Follow the steps at left for a fried egg center you'll flip over!

15

Cowgirl Lunch

It's high noon, so round up your appetite and spread out your bandanna for a southwestern-style meal.

Burrito Sandwich

YOU WILL NEED

Ingredients
- 1 large leaf of lettuce
- 1 medium tomato
- 1 flour tortilla
- 1 teaspoon Thousand Island dressing or mayonnaise
- 3 thin slices of turkey or chicken breast
- 2 teaspoons of guacamole
- 2 tablespoons of shredded Colby or Monterey Jack cheese

Equipment
- Paper towels
- Measuring spoons
- Spoon and butter knife
- Sharp knife
- Cutting board
- String or twine
- Plastic wrap

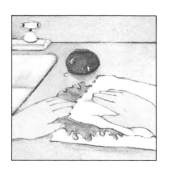

1 Wash the lettuce and tomato in cold water. Pat dry with the paper towels.

2 Spread the tortilla evenly with the dressing or mayonnaise. Place the lettuce leaf on top. If necessary, trim off any edges that hang over the sides.

3 Lay the turkey or chicken on top of the lettuce. Cut 2 thin slices of tomato. Arrange them on top of the meat.

4 Spoon on the guacamole. Then sprinkle the cheese over the guacamole.

5 To roll up the tortilla, carefully fold one side in toward the middle. Then wrap the other side up around it tightly to close.

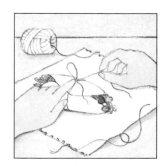

6 Use string to tie a bow around the sandwich. (A knot is harder to undo.) Wrap it in plastic wrap.

Another Twist: For an all-veggie version, build your burrito out of bean dip, sliced avocado, lettuce, tomato, and cheese.

Chocolate Canyon Pudding

For a sweet dessert with south-of-the-border zip, bring along some grated coconut and a dash of cinnamon to add to a chocolate pudding cup.

Yee-ha...ahhh!

After herding cattle all morning, take a swig of some fresh, cold milk.

And don't forget a sweet, juicy apple for your hardworking horse!

Nacho Popcorn

Brand it yourself! Melt 1 tablespoon of margarine or butter. Then stir in ¼ teaspoon of taco seasoning mix. Put the mixture in a plastic bag with 4 cups of cheese popcorn, close the bag tightly, and shake. Take a scoopful for lunch and save the rest for later, when you're snacking back at the ranch.

Safari Lunch

Eat on the wild side! Take all the food and supplies you'll need for this amazing animal adventure.

Wild Turkey Sandwich

YOU WILL NEED

Ingredients
- 1 stalk of celery
- 1 tablespoon of dried cranberries or raisins
- 2 tablespoons of soft cream cheese
- 1½ tablespoons of mayonnaise
- 3 ounces (¾ cup) of cooked turkey
- 1 slice of dark bread
- 1 slice of light bread

Equipment
- Sharp knife
- Cutting board
- Measuring cup and spoons
- Mixing bowl
- Spoon

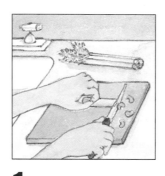

1 Wash the celery. Chop it into small pieces.

2 Combine 1 tablespoon of chopped celery with the dried fruit, cream cheese, and 1 tablespoon of mayonnaise.

3 Chop the turkey into small pieces. Add it to the mixture.

4 Spread each slice of bread with the remaining mayonnaise. Spoon turkey salad onto one slice and place the other on top. Put any leftover salad in the refrigerator, covered, for later.

5 Cut the sandwich into 4 or 5 strips, each about ½–1 inch wide.

6 Carefully flip over the first strip so the different-colored bread shows. Skip the second strip, then turn over the third. Keep going, skipping every other strip.

Feeding Time

Don't forget a banana for the monkey, peanuts for the elephant, broccoli "treetops" for the giraffe, and a cold drink from the nearest watering hole.

19

Grab Bags to Go

Alphabet Lunch

Pick a letter—any letter! Then think of foods that begin with that letter. For example, please pass the P's: Parmesan pasta salad with peppers and peas; a pile of pretzels, potato chips, pistachio nuts, and pumpkin seeds; a pear; a pink drink; and some peppermint candies.

Big Sis–Little Sis Lunch

Got a younger sister who wants to be just like you? Treat her to a mini version of your meal. Or bring the small-sized samples to trade with a friend.

Try these themes or dream up one of your own!

Fun-Day Lunch

Celebrate a birthday, toast a team victory, or turn an anyday lunch into a fabulous feast! To make the sandwiches, cut the bread, meat, and cheese with star-shaped cookie cutters. To make celery fans, cut slits in celery sticks and refrigerate them overnight in water. For a party favor, roll up a cellophane-wrapped stack of crackers or cookies in a napkin. Tie the ends.

Polka-Dot Lunch

Here's a lunch that's centered around circles, including a "hole" bagel sandwich made with vegetable cream cheese and slices of raw veggies.

Mix 'n' Match Handfuls

Sweet Sensations

Satisfy your sweet tooth with dried fruit, cereal, and maybe just a few of your favorite candy morsels.

Can't decide on a snack? Mix a little of each—sweet, salty, crunchy, chewy, nutty, fruity—all in one bowl.

Savory Flavors

Nuts, seeds, crispy chips, mini crackers, and more— they're all fun to munch on!

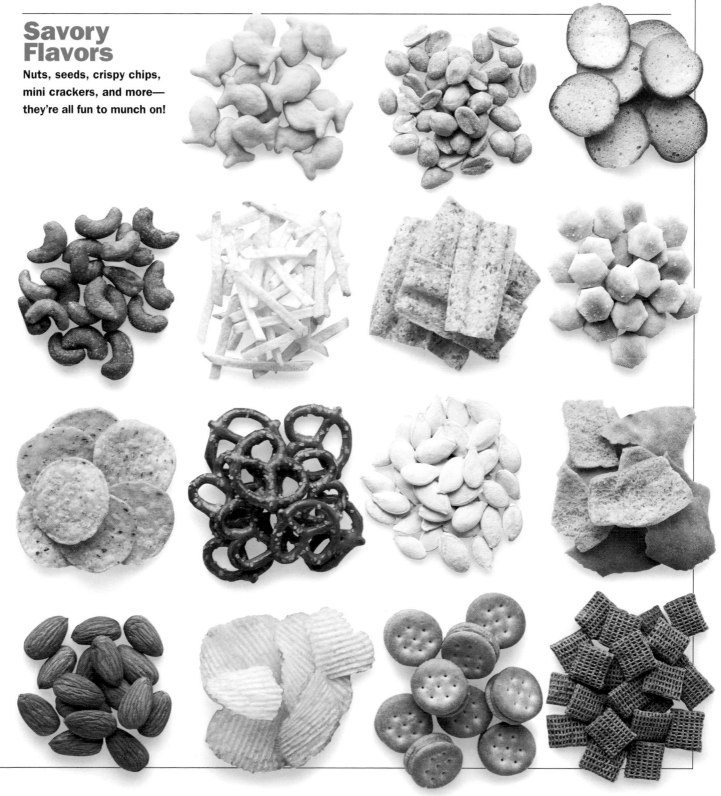

Warm Up, Cool Down!

Red-Hot Chocolate

In a microwave-safe measuring cup, combine ¾ cup of water and 6 Red Hots. Microwave on HIGH for 2 minutes. Empty 1 packet of instant cocoa with marshmallows into a mug. Pour the hot mixture over it and stir well. Add whipped topping and more Red Hots.

Tea-rrific

Place 1 teabag in a mug. Pour 1 cup of boiling water into it and let it steep until the tea is the strength you like. Then remove the bag. Spoon in 2 teaspoons of sweetened powdered drink mix, such as Kool-Aid® or Tang™. Stir the drink with a candy stick.

Mulled Apple Cider

In a small saucepan, combine 1 cup of apple juice or cider, 1 teaspoon of brown sugar, 1 orange slice, and a dash of cinnamon, nutmeg, allspice, and ground cloves. Heat the mixture on the stove until it boils. Then turn the heat down and simmer with the cover on for 10 minutes. Ladle the cider into a mug and stir with a cinnamon stick.

Melt away the day with a mug of steamy, hot sweetness. Or chill out with something fresh and fruity.

Apple Peach Blossom

Peel 1 fresh peach. Cut it into thin slices. Place the slices in a plastic zipper-top bag, lying flat. Put the bag in the freezer for 1–2 hours. Then remove $\frac{1}{4}$ of the slices and break them into pieces. Combine in a blender with $\frac{1}{3}$ cup of milk and $\frac{1}{4}$ cup of frozen apple juice concentrate. Cover and blend until smooth. Pour into a glass, and add more peach slices for fruity ice cubes!

Fruit Smoothy

Cut up 4 strawberries and half a banana. Combine the fruit in a blender with $\frac{1}{2}$ cup of tropical fruit drink and 1 scoop of vanilla or strawberry frozen yogurt. Cover and blend on LOW until smooth, then on HIGH to make it foamy.

Lemonade Fizz

Cut a slice of lemon. Then use a juicer to squeeze the juice out of the rest of the lemon. Remove the seeds. Then pour the juice into a glass. Stir in about 5 teaspoons of sugar and $1\frac{1}{4}$ cups of club soda. Add ice cubes and the lemon slice.

Spaghetti Pie

Any way you slice it, this spaghetti is as easy as pie!

YOU WILL NEED

An adult to help you

Ingredients
- ¼ teaspoon of salt
- ½ teaspoon of vegetable oil
- ½ pound of spaghetti
- 1 egg
- ⅓ cup of grated Parmesan cheese
- 1 tablespoon of soft butter or margarine
- Dab of shortening
- Half an onion
- Half a green pepper
- ½ pound of ground beef
- 1 cup of spaghetti sauce
- ¾ cup of ricotta or cottage cheese
- ½ cup of shredded mozzarella cheese

Equipment
- Measuring cups and spoons
- 2-quart saucepan
- Colander
- 2 forks, mixing spoon
- Medium mixing bowl
- Paper towel
- 9-inch pie plate
- Knife, cutting board
- Skillet
- Oven mitts
- Cooling rack

1 Boil 2 quarts of water. Add the salt, oil, and spaghetti. Then boil for 8–10 minutes, stirring occasionally. With an adult, use the colander to drain and rinse the spaghetti in cold water.

2 Use a fork to beat together the egg, Parmesan cheese, and butter or margarine in the mixing bowl. Add the spaghetti and use 2 forks to toss until evenly mixed.

3 Use a paper towel to grease the pie plate with shortening. Then spoon the spaghetti mixture into the pie plate. Press the mixture to the sides and bottom to mold it to the shape of the plate.

4 Chop up the onion and green pepper. In the skillet, cook ½ cup of the onion and ¼ cup of the green pepper with the ground beef over medium heat. When brown, have an adult help you drain off the fat. Then add the spaghetti sauce.

5 Preheat the oven to 350 degrees. Spoon the ricotta or cottage cheese into the pie "crust" and spread it evenly around the bottom. Then add the meat sauce. Bake the pie for 30–35 minutes.

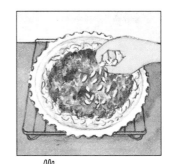

6 When the pie is done, use the oven mitts to take the pie out of the oven and place on a cooling rack. Sprinkle the pie with the shredded cheese. Let cool for 10 minutes before serving.

Do-It-Yourself Dressing

Toss a side salad with this tasty Italian-style dressing.

Makes about 15 servings

You will need:

Ingredients
- 1 garlic clove
- ⅔ cup of vegetable oil
- ⅓ cup of red wine vinegar
- ½ teaspoon of Dijon mustard
- ¼ teaspoon of premixed Italian seasoning, or a combination of oregano, basil, onion powder, and salt

Equipment
- Garlic press or knife
- Measuring cup and spoons
- Jar with a tight-fitting lid

1 Crush the garlic clove in the garlic press. Or use a knife to split the clove in half.

2 Put the garlic in the jar with the other ingredients.

3 Screw the lid on tightly and shake well. Store in the refrigerator. Remove any large garlic pieces before serving.

1 Potato, 2 Potato

It's easy to turn a so-so side dish into a mouth-watering main course.

Baked in the Oven

YOU WILL NEED

An adult to help you

Ingredients
- 1 potato
- Softened butter or vegetable oil

Equipment
- Vegetable scrubber
- Fork
- Oven mitt

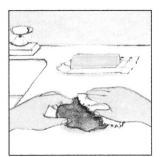

1 Preheat the oven to 400 degrees. Scrub and dry the potato. Then rub it with the butter or oil.

2 Prick the skin several times with the fork to allow steam to escape while cooking. (Otherwise the potato might burst.) Place the potato right on the oven rack and bake for about an hour.

3 To tell if the potato is done, put on an oven mitt and squeeze the potato. If it is slightly soft, or if you can pierce it easily with a fork, it's cooked.

. . . or the Microwave

YOU WILL NEED

Ingredients
- 1 potato

Equipment
- Vegetable scrubber
- Fork
- Paper towel
- Clean dish towel
- Oven mitt

1 Scrub and dry the potato. Pierce holes in it with the fork.

2 Place the potato on a paper towel. Microwave on HIGH for 2 minutes. Turn the potato over and microwave on HIGH for another 2–4 minutes.

3 Remove the potato from the microwave and wrap it in the dish towel. Let it stand a few minutes to allow the potato to continue cooking.

Mexican Potato

Split a baked potato in half and fill it with a combination of shredded Colby and Monterey Jack cheese, chopped tomato, and salsa. Top it off with sour cream and guacamole.

Creamy Veggie Potato

In a covered casserole dish, combine a 10-ounce package of frozen broccoli and cheese sauce with 1 cup of frozen peas and carrots. Microwave on HIGH for 4–6 minutes, stirring once. Split a baked potato in half and spoon some vegetable mixture over each half. You'll have enough left over to make another potato or to serve as a side dish at another meal.

Chili Tater Dog

Split a baked potato lengthwise down the middle. Place a hot dog in the middle and top with 2 tablespoons of chili. Cover loosely with waxed paper or plastic wrap and microwave on HIGH for about 1½ minutes. Sprinkle with shredded cheddar cheese.

Pizza Your Way

Experiment with different crusts and fixings to find the pizza that's perfect for you.

Popeye Pizza

✋ Drain a can of Italian-style stewed tomatoes. Spread them on a round *focaccia* (Italian flat bread), such as Boboli®. Add cooked spinach, red peppers, bacon, and shredded mozzarella cheese. Place on a cookie sheet and bake at 425 degrees for 8–10 minutes.

Pizza Sub

✋💚 Spread pizza sauce on half of a loaf of Italian bread. Sprinkle with Italian seasoning. Top with ham, pepperoni, salami, green pepper, and slices of mozzarella, cheddar, and American cheeses. Bake at 425 degrees for 8–10 minutes.

Pizza with Personality

Need more ideas? Pick from these possibilities:

Crusts
- Bagel
- Pita bread
- English muffln

Sauces
- Spaghetti sauce
- Barbecue sauce
- Pesto

Cheeses
- Provolone
- Muenster
- Feta
- Ricotta

Toppings
- Zucchini
- Grilled chicken
- Eggplant
- Canadian bacon
- Artichoke hearts
- Hot dog slices
- Broccoli
- Olives
- Sunflower seeds

Pizza Olé!

✋💚 In a skillet, cook ground beef with a little taco seasoning. Use a fork to poke holes in a flour tortilla. Wet your hands and pat both sides of the tortilla. Place it between 2 paper towels and microwave on HIGH 45–60 seconds, until almost crisp. Remove the paper towels. Add ground beef and shredded Colby and Monterey Jack cheese. Microwave on HIGH 1–1½ minutes. Top with lettuce, sour cream, and salsa.

Potted Pudding

Look what's springing up! You don't need a green thumb to grow this delicious dessert.

YOU WILL NEED

An adult to help you

Ingredients
- 1 pound of chocolate sandwich cookies, such as Oreos®
- 8 ounces of cream cheese, softened
- ¼ cup of margarine, softened
- ¼ cup of powdered sugar
- 12 ounces of Cool Whip®, thawed
- 3 cups of milk
- 2 packages of instant vanilla pudding
- Gummi Worms

Equipment
- Clean, new flowerpot, large enough to hold 2½–3 quarts
- Plastic wrap
- Zipper-top plastic bag
- Rolling pin
- 2 large mixing bowls
- Electric mixer
- Rubber spatula
- Spoon and wire whisk
- Fake flowers

1 Use plastic wrap to plug up the hole at the bottom of the flowerpot.

2 Fill the zipper-top bag with as many cookies as will fit. Use the rolling pin to crush the cookies into crumbs. Add more cookies and crush them. Repeat until you have crushed all of the cookies.

3 Combine the cream cheese, margarine, and sugar in a mixing bowl. Beat with the mixer on MEDIUM until fluffy. Add the Cool Whip and beat on LOW until smooth, scraping the sides with the spatula.

4 In the other bowl, combine the milk and instant pudding. Use the wire whisk or spoon to blend until slightly thick. Add this mixture to the cream cheese mixture and blend until smooth.

5 Pour about a third of the cookie crumbs into the bottom of the flowerpot. Then spoon in half the pudding mixture. Add another layer of cookie crumbs, then the rest of the pudding mixture.

6 Sprinkle the remaining cookie crumbs on top. Cover and refrigerate for several hours or overnight. Then decorate with candy worms and fake flowers.

Dig In!

Your friends will be amazed when you dish out each serving with a garden trowel.

Less-Mess Cake

One pan + one plastic bag = one very delicious cake!
You'll have lots of fun—not lots of messy kitchen cleanup.

YOU WILL NEED

An adult to help you

Ingredients

- 1½ cups of flour
- 1 cup of sugar
- 3 heaping tablespoons of unsweetened cocoa
- 1 teaspoon of baking soda
- ½ teaspoon of salt
- 6 tablespoons of vegetable oil
- 1 tablespoon of white vinegar
- 1 teaspoon of vanilla
- 1 cup of cold water

Equipment

- Measuring cups and spoons
- 8-inch square pan or 9-inch round pan
- Fork, knife, and spoon
- Toothpick
- Oven mitts
- Cooling rack
- Plate

1 Preheat the oven to 350 degrees. Measure the flour, sugar, cocoa, baking soda, and salt into the pan. Mix well with the fork.

2 Make 3 holes in the dry mixture. Pour the oil into 1 hole, the vinegar into another hole, and the vanilla into the last hole.

3 Carefully add the cold water and mix everything together with the fork. Be sure to mix thoroughly so the dry ingredients don't stick to the sides and bottom of the pan.

4 Put the pan on the middle rack in the oven. Bake 35–40 minutes, or until a toothpick poked into the center of the cake comes out clean.

5 Using the mitts, remove the cake from the oven and place it on the cooling rack. Let the cake cool in the pan for about 35 minutes.

6 Run the knife around the outside of the cake, separating it from the pan. Turn the pan upside down on the plate. Tap the back of the pan with the spoon to loosen the cake. Lift off. Let the cake cool completely.

Squeeze out swirls, squiggles, or simple straight lines. Frost your cake with flair!

Squish 'n' Squeeze Frosting

You will need:

Ingredients
- 1 cup of powdered sugar
- 4½ teaspoons of milk
- ¼ teaspoon of vanilla

Equipment
- Measuring cup and spoons
- Quart-size zipper-top bag
- Plate
- Scissors

1 Pour the sugar into the bag. Pour the milk and vanilla into the bag and seal it. Squish the bag with your hands for about 2 minutes until the frosting is smooth.

2 Place a plate over the cooled cake, and flip the cake over so it's right side up.

3 Squeeze the frosting down to 1 corner of the bag. Cut the tip off the corner with scissors. Squeeze the frosting over the cake, as shown below.

Flower Cookies

These bright blossoms have a sweet surprise inside. Share them with a friend on a rainy day.

YOU WILL NEED

An adult to help you

Ingredients

- 1 stick (½ cup) of butter, softened
- ¼ cup of light brown sugar, firmly packed
- 1 cup of flour
- 12 bite-size candy bars without nuts

Equipment

- Measuring cups and spoons
- Mixing bowl
- Mixing spoon
- Cookie sheet
- Aluminum foil
- 12 wooden craft sticks

1 Preheat the oven to 325 degrees. In the mixing bowl, stir the butter and brown sugar together until blended.

2 Stir in the flour. Form the dough into a ball in the bowl with your hands. If the dough is sticky, stir in more flour, 1 tablespoon at a time.

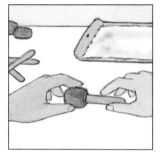

3 Cover the cookie sheet with a piece of aluminum foil. Unwrap the candy bars. Insert a stick into the side of each candy bar.

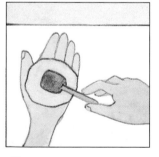

4 Place a tablespoon of dough in the palm of your hand. Flatten it into a disk. Place one of the candies on a stick in the center of the dough disk.

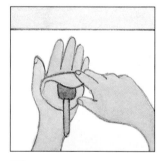

5 Wrap the dough completely around the candy. Make the other pops the same way. Place them on the cookie sheet. Slightly flatten each pop with the palm of your hand.

6 Bake the cookies 18–20 minutes, until the edges are golden. If the cookies split open while they bake, gently press the edges together while they are cooling. Let them cool completely. Then decorate with petals, following the directions at right.

Pretty Petals

You will need:

Ingredients
- 15 large marshmallows
- 1 tube of icing, any color
- 1 tube of yellow icing

Equipment
- Scissors or kitchen shears
- 2⅓ yards of green ribbon
- Ruler

1 Wash the scissors and dry them. Snip each marshmallow into 4 slices, as shown.

2 Cover the face of each cookie with colored icing. Carefully press 5 marshmallow slices into the frosting to look like flower petals. Fill the center with a dab of yellow icing.

3 Cut 7-inch pieces of ribbon. Tie them around each stick to look like leaves.

Celebrate!

Homemade Valentines

Floating hearts, frosted cookies, fruity things to drink— There's just one rule: color it all pink!

Magic Heart Parfaits

Serves 4

You will need:

♥ An adult to help you

Ingredients

- .28-ounce-size Kool-Aid® pink lemonade mix
- 1 cup of sugar
- 4 envelopes of Knox® unflavored gelatin
- 4 red Gummi Hearts or Red Hot Dollars®, found at grocery and candy stores
- Whipped topping
- Candy sprinkles

Equipment

- Measuring cup
- Pitcher and long spoon
- Saucepan
- 4 parfait glasses or tall drinking glasses
- Waxed paper
- Rolling pin or heavy can
- Scissors or small heart-shaped cookie cutter

1 In the pitcher, mix the lemonade and sugar as directed on the package.

2 ♥ Prepare the gelatin according to the Knox Blox recipe, using lemonade instead of juice. Then pour into each glass. Refrigerate for 50 minutes.

3 If you couldn't find candy hearts, make your own with Red Hot Dollars while you're waiting for the gelatin to set. Place 1 Dollar between 2 pieces of waxed paper. Roll with the rolling pin or can until the candy is about ⅛ inch thick. Use the scissors or cookie cutter to cut hearts out of the candy.

4 After 50 minutes, see if the gelatin is partially set. You should be able to stick your finger into it, but it should feel thick and heavy.

5 When the gelatin is partially set, push 1 heart into each glass. If the hearts sink to the bottom, the gelatin isn't ready. Take out the hearts and chill the glasses for another 5 minutes, then try again.

6 Put the glasses with hearts in them back in the refrigerator for 30 minutes or until the gelatin is completely set. Top with whipped topping and candy sprinkles.

Lovable Cookies

Makes 15 cookies

You will need:

🤚❤️ An adult to help you

Ingredients

- 1 chilled 20-ounce roll of prepared sugar-cookie dough, such as Pillsbury
- 1 16-ounce can of pink frosting
- Powdered sugar

Equipment

- Rolling pin
- Waxed paper
- Heart-shaped cookie cutters
- Table knife
- Cookie sheet

1 Prepare the cookie dough according to the directions for rolled cookies.

2 Cut hearts in the dough with the cookie cutter. With a knife or smaller cookie cutter, cut out another heart in the center of half the cookies.

3 🤚❤️ Place on the cookie sheet and bake at 350 degrees for 7–9 minutes. You can bake the baby hearts, too, but for only 5 minutes! Let cool.

4 Frost each big solid cookie. Sprinkle powdered sugar on each cutout cookie and place on top.

Sweetheart Slushies

Serves 4

You will need:

🤚❤️ An adult to help you

Ingredients

- 2 cups of ice cubes
- 8 ounces of frozen raspberries
- 2 tablespoons of sugar
- ¼ cup of water

Equipment

- Measuring cups and spoon
- Blender
- 4 tall glasses
- Straws and pink ribbon

1 🤚❤️ Have an adult help you mix the ice cubes, raspberries, and sugar in the blender for 3 minutes.

2 🤚❤️ Add the water and blend for 2 more minutes.

3 Pour into the glasses. Serve with straws tied with pink bows!

Tricky Treats

Don't let the Halloween hungries get you!

Creepy Crawly Cookies

You will need:

🖐 An adult to help you

Ingredients

- 2 cups chocolate chips
- ½ cup crispy rice cereal
- ¼ cup shredded coconut
- 1½ cups chow mein noodles
- Ready-made tube icing

Equipment

- Measuring cups
- Heavy saucepan, spoon
- Waxed paper

1 🖐 Melt 1 cup of the chocolate chips in the saucepan over low heat.

2 Mix in the cereal and coconut. Drop spoonfuls of the mixture onto waxed paper to make bug bodies.

3 🖐 Melt the second cup of chocolate chips. Stir in the noodles.

4 Let cool, then carefully pick out the noodles and stick them to the bodies. Add dots of icing for eyes.

Orange-O'-Lantern

You will need:

🖐 An adult to help you

Ingredients

- Orange
- 1 cup of ice cream or sherbet
- Cinnamon stick

Equipment

- Sharp knife
- Spoon

1 🖐 Cut the top off an orange. Scoop out the fruit. Carve the orange as if it were a pumpkin.

2 Fill the orange with the ice cream or sherbet.

3 Cut a hole in the top and stick a short piece of cinnamon stick in it.

Popcorn Witch

You will need:

Ingredients

- Popcorn ball
- Black licorice whips
- Ready-made tube icing

Equipment

- Scissors, tape
- Black construction paper
- Toothpicks
- Orange yarn

1 Cut a strip of paper and tape it into a circle. Set the popcorn ball on the circle.

2 Drape the licorice whips over the popcorn ball for hair. Secure with toothpicks.

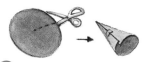

3 Cut out a paper circle. Cut a slit from the edge to the center. Roll it into a cone and tape the edge.

4 Cut out a doughnut-shaped brim. Tape the cone to the brim. Add a band of orange yarn.

5 Use the icing to make a mouth and eyes.

Can you *trick* your friends into eating an insect? You might—if you *treat* them to this Halloween party with lots of spooky food! Serve a witchy brew of orange soda to your guests. And don't forget to slip the witch's black cat over each straw!

Celebrate!

Sleepover Pleasers

These slumber party treats are a guaranteed cure for the midnight munchies.

S'nore-zzz

Everyone adores s'mores, and your guests will love these new combos even more! Stack the filling on a graham cracker with the marshmallow last. Place on a plate, not exactly in the center. Microwave on HIGH 15–20 seconds, until the marshmallow puffs up. Add the top cracker and press down. Let cool before eating.

Cinnamon-Chocolate-Peanut Butter S'nore

- 2 cinnamon graham cracker squares
- 1 chocolate-peanut butter candy cup
- 1 marshmallow

Chocolate-Banana S'nore

- 2 regular graham cracker squares
- $\frac{1}{3}$ of a chocolate bar
- 2 thin slices of banana
- 1 marshmallow

Bowl your guests over with tasty popcorn combos, such as plain, caramel, and cheddar!

Chocolate-Raspberry-Peanut Butter S'nore

- 2 chocolate-flavored graham cracker squares
- A smear of peanut butter
- A dab of raspberry preserves
- 1 marshmallow

Poppin' Toppings

Shake up plain old popcorn with easy add-on ingredients! Try Parmesan cheese, garlic salt and butter, spicy Cajun pepper, or cinnamon and sugar. Mix up a batch of each for your guests to sample—then have everyone vote on her favorite kind.

Sweet Dreams

All you need are graham crackers and frosting to make these happy campers. Let each guest decorate her own.

43

Frosty Holiday Scene

Make a delicious decoration with cookies, candy, and frosting!

Getting Started

Use this frosting to join the pieces of your houses and trees. The raw eggs make the frosting good for gluing but not eating!

YOU WILL NEED

An adult to help you

Ingredients
- 2 large eggs
- 4 cups of powdered sugar

Equipment
- Mixing bowl
- Electric mixer
- Measuring cup
- Spoon
- Squeeze bottle— an empty ketchup dispenser works well

1 Have an adult help you separate the egg whites from the 2 eggs. Put the whites into a mixing bowl.

2 With a mixer, beat the whites until they form peaks when you lift the beaters.

3 Mix in 3 cups of the powdered sugar. Slowly add more sugar to make the frosting thick, but not too thick to squeeze out of the bottle. Spoon the frosting into the squeeze bottle.

Build a House

Make a basic house, then use your imagination for decorating ideas!

1 Rinse out the milk carton and let it dry. Staple the spout closed.

2 Trim 4 graham cracker squares if necessary to make them fit on the sides of the carton. (Nibbling is an easy way to trim them!) Squeeze a layer of frosting onto 1 graham cracker. Press it to 1 side of the carton. Repeat on all sides.

3 Squeeze a thick layer of frosting onto 1 side of 2 graham cracker squares. Press them onto the top of the carton for the roof.

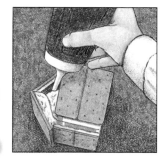

4 Squeeze frosting to fill in the triangle-shaped spaces of the milk carton at the front and back of the roof.

5 Squeeze a thick stripe of frosting to fill in each corner of the house. Press licorice or candy sticks into the frosting.

6 Use frosting to attach candy to the roof. Add more candy to make a door, a chimney, windows, and bushes. Let the house dry overnight.

Grow Some Greenery

Use ice-cream cones to create a forest of evergreen trees for your winter wonderland!

YOU WILL NEED

- ♥ **An adult to help you**
- ■ **Bag of spearmint-leaf candy**
- ■ **Table knife**
- ■ **Sugar cones**
- ■ **Squeeze bottle filled with frosting**

1 ♥ To make a tree, slice about 12 spearmint-leaf candies in half so they are half as thick. Each candy will give you 2 thin leaves.

2 Turn an ice-cream cone upside down. Cover the entire cone with frosting. Then, starting at the bottom, press a row of leaves into the frosting. Add more rows of leaves, overlapping the rows as you move up the cone.

3 You can make smaller trees by using only part of a cone. Break or nibble off the wide end of 1 cone to get the size you want. Then follow Step 2. Let your trees dry overnight.

Add Finishing Touches

Complete your scene with a fence, a path, and flaky snow.

YOU WILL NEED

- ■ **Heavy cardboard**
- ■ **Squeeze bottle filled with frosting**
- ■ **Mini pretzel twists**
- ■ **Plain M&M's candy**
- ■ **M&M's Mini Baking Bits**
- ■ **Bag of shredded coconut**

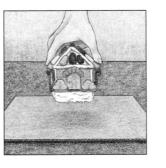

1 Arrange your finished houses and trees on a piece of cardboard large enough to hold them all. Use frosting to attach each house and tree to the base.

2 To make a fence, attach pretzels to the base with dots of frosting. To make a sidewalk, draw a path with frosting. Press M&M's and mini M&M's into the path.

3 Sprinkle coconut over the whole scene to look like snow.

Terms & Tools

What's the difference between boiling and broiling? Between a skillet and a saucepan? Learn your lingo.

What to Do

Bake
To cook in the oven.

Beat
To mix with a fast, stirring motion, using a wire whisk, fork, eggbeater, or electric mixer.

Boil
To heat liquid until large bubbles keep rising and bursting on the surface.

Broil
To brown very quickly in the oven, with all of the heat coming down from above the food.

Chop
To cut into small, uneven pieces.

Dice
To cut into tiny squares.

Grate
To rub against the rough, sharp surface of a grater, making shreds.

Peel
To remove skin from vegetables or fruit with a peeler, a knife, or fingers.

Sauté
To cook quickly and lightly in a skillet with a little butter or oil.

Simmer
To cook for a while on the stove, allowing the liquid to stay hot and slowly form bubbles but not boil.

Steam
To place in a container over boiling water, allowing the steam to cook the food.

What to Use

casserole

measuring spoons

spatulas

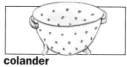
colander

mixing bowls

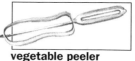
utility knife

garlic press

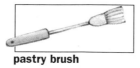
pastry brush

vegetable peeler

ice cream scoop

saucepan

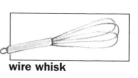
vegetable scrubber

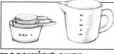
measuring cups

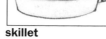
skillet

wire whisk